THE GHOSTLY TALES OF ATCHISON

Published by Arcadia Children's Books
A Division of Arcadia Publishing, Inc.
Charleston, SC
www.arcadiapublishing.com

First published 2024
Manufactured in the United States

Designed by Jessica Nevins
Images used courtesy of Shutterstock.com; p. 8 Atchison County Historical Society; p. 48 Ammodramus/File:Amelia Earhart birthplace from NE 1.JPG/Wikimedia Commons/CC0; p. 104 Mystic Stock Photography/hutterstock.com.

ISBN: 9781467196000
Library of Congress Control Number: 2025932961

Spooky America

THE GHOSTLY TALES OF ATCHISON

BROOKE MONTOYA

Adapted from *Haunted Atchison* by Brooke Montoya

arcadia CHILDREN'S BOOKS

Nebraska
Iowa
Colorado
Kansas
Missouri
New Mexico
Oklahoma
Texas
Arkansas
11
8
3
1
6
5
10
9
7
20
16
15
14
13
12
18
17
4
2
19
Atchison

Table of Contents & Map Key

Atchison, Kansas

Welcome to Spooky Atchison!

Have you ever wondered why we see, hear, and experience ghosts? I have spent the last ten years traveling to different places in America, hoping to answer that question. Curiosities about ghosts led me to the city of Atchison, a city in the far northeast corner of Kansas, on the banks of the Missouri River. (In fact, if you cross the Amelia Earhart Bridge and drive over the river, you will be in Missouri.) Atchison claims to be the "most haunted city in Kansas." But why is Atchison so haunted? How could such a small city have so many ghost stories? Once I visited the city and saw for myself, I became a believer.

This book's ghostly tales are collected from my own experiences, as well as newspapers, books, and stories of people who have experienced unexplainable things. The stories go all the way back to when the city was home to Indigenous peoples, known as the Kanza. Arrowheads, bones, and remains of their villages were found all over Atchison when the city was being built in the late 1850s.

Other ghostly tales come from the end of the nineteenth century, when Atchison was part of the Wild West. People came from states back East and from around the world to be a part of the westward expansion in the United States. Many of Atchison's first settlers had important jobs in town as lawyers, doctors, or politicians, and they built their gorgeous homes for their families. Many of the wealthy people who lived in Atchison knew each other and spent time together.

One theory about why Atchison is so haunted is that these early settlers often came to Atchison from other places with very little, built a better life for themselves, and never

wanted to leave. That's right . . . even after they died.

Another group of people who came through Atchison were the Mormons. They passed through the city on their way to Utah. When Atchison was first founded, many Mormons and other residents became sick and died of disease. Diseases spread easily when people would travel to new locations, and cholera, Spanish flu, and (later) tuberculosis killed many people in Atchison. In those days, doctors did not have medications to help fight or cure illnesses, so many died. Sometimes, families would lose multiple family members to a disease. The loss was heartbreaking and may have contributed to the number of restless souls still wandering around today.

The tales I've collected here are sure to keep you sleeping with the light on *and* tucking your toes extra tightly under the blanket while you sleep. Stories of haunted restaurants, houses where the residents refuse to leave, ghosts that still call out from the Missouri River, and many others. Ghosts can be scary, but remember, they were living people once, with families, jobs, hobbies, and a favorite ice cream flavor. Many ghosts just want their stories to be told and for people to know that their lives mattered. And they *do* matter. So, enjoy their stories, and the next time you walk around Atchison, keep your eyes and ears open for a ghostly encounter!

Part One

Haunted Historical Houses

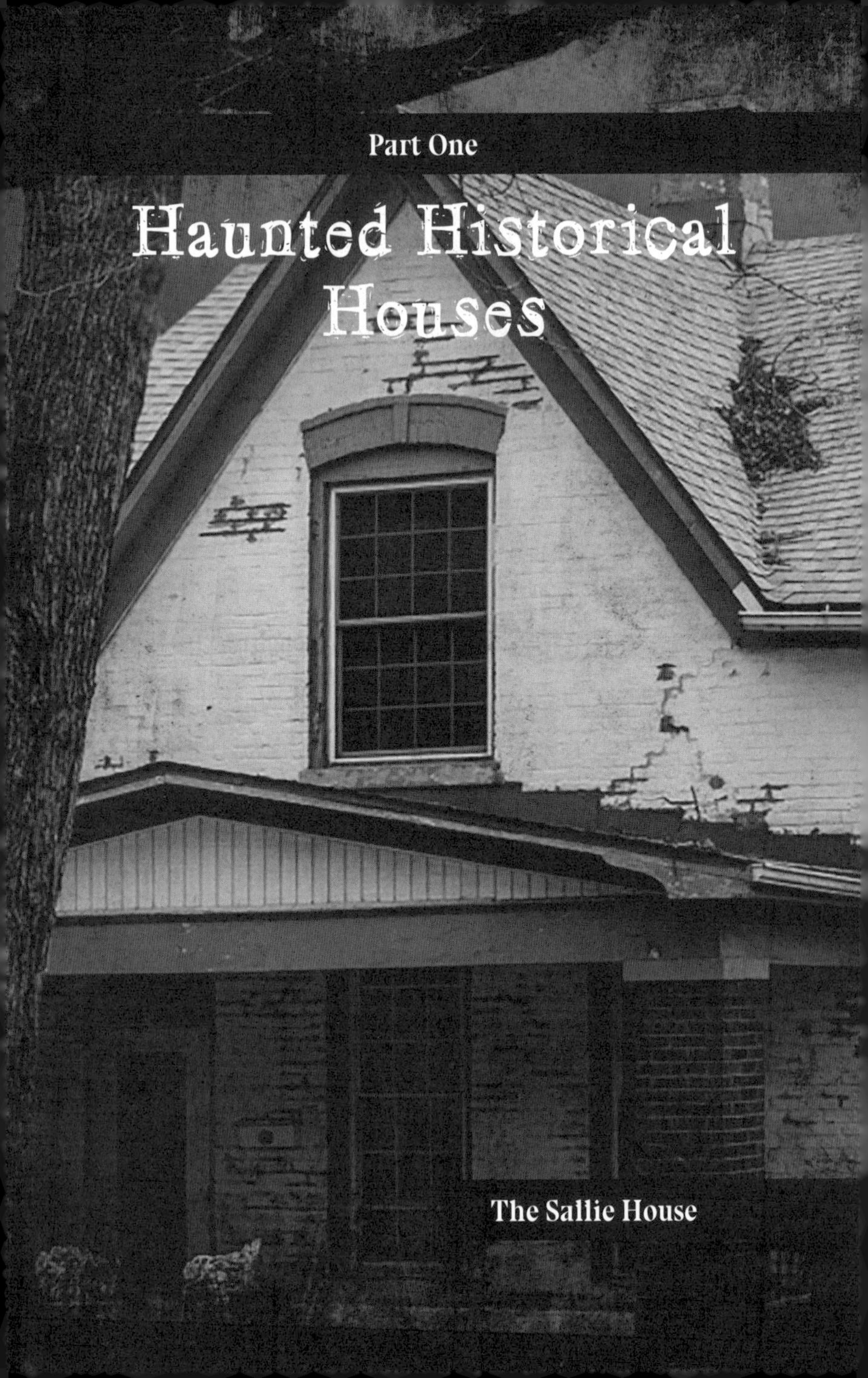

The Sallie House

CHAPTER 1

Sallie House

On Second Street, in the older part of Atchison, sits a small white house. Looking at the house, you might not think ghosts live inside. After all, many of the houses in Atchison are not what we picture in our minds when we think of a haunted house. But there are ghosts waiting to reach out and talk to people who dare to enter.

The house, now called the Sallie House, got its name from the little girl who is thought to still haunt the house today. Many think Sallie was around six years old. One rainy night, she awoke with terrible stomach pain. Hospitals were not as common as they are today, so her mother carried her to a neighbor who was a children's doctor. This doctor may have been Charles Finney, who grew up in the small white house on Second Street. He lived in the red house next door, but for a bit he saw patients at his childhood home. Sallie's mother frantically knocked on the doctor's door pleading for his help. The story is told that the doctor had to do an emergency surgery on Sallie to remove her appendix. Tragically, she died during the surgery.

Many believe this to be the same Sallie whose ghost haunts the house—and that she may be angry at the doctor for not saving her.

Others think that perhaps she is looking for her mother because she does not know she died. Though there is no evidence that a little girl named Sallie ever died in the house on Second Street, that does not necessarily mean the story isn't true. Like all things supernatural, you will have to decide for yourself!

The Mize family lived in the white house on Second Street in the early 1990s. Heather Mize had an imaginary friend she would play with in her room. Heather told her parents her imaginary friend was named Sallie. But what her parents didn't realize was that Sallie wasn't imaginary at all—she was a ghost!

After the Mize family moved out, Deborah and Tony Pickman, and their baby Taylor, moved into the home in 1992. During the year that the Pickman family lived there, they saw the ghost of a little girl throughout the house. She wore a blue dress and had curly pigtails with bows in her hair. The family's dog would often bark wildly at empty corners of rooms, his eyes following something invisible moving across the walls. Lights would flicker on and off by themselves, especially at night when everyone was trying to sleep. Sometimes all the lights in the house would suddenly turn on in the middle of the night, waking everyone up!

Once, when the family had gone out to dinner, they returned home and found something interesting and a bit eerie. All the baby's stuffed animals had been placed on the floor of the nursery in a circle. Nobody had been home when this happened. The family was sure that the little girl ghost had done this with the toys. In fact, the things she did frightened the family so much, they moved out.

Today, the Sallie House is open to anyone who wants to come in and see if they can talk to a ghost. You can walk through the house during the day, or sleep inside overnight. Visitors often report cold spots that suddenly appear in rooms, making their breath visible even on warm days. Electronic devices like phones and cameras mysteriously drain their batteries within minutes. Some people have even felt tiny fingers tugging at their clothes, or heard the faint sound of a child's laughter echoing from empty rooms.

So, what do you think? Are you brave enough to come and talk to the ghostly girl with the curly pigtails? Just don't be surprised if she decides to rearrange your belongings while you're not looking!

CHAPTER 2

Price Boulevard

A two-story house that sits at 936 Price Boulevard holds a terrifying tale from an event in 1989. However, it also shares a history with the Zibold-Haegelin Brewery that once sat across the street in the 1890s. Buckle your seat belt for this twisty tale!

In 1989, Larry Sarvey moved to Atchison from New York City with his wife Kathy and their two children to work for the newspaper the *Atchison Globe*. When Kathy and Larry got divorced, Kathy moved back to New York with the children. Larry started dating a woman named Sandi who worked at the newspaper with him. Sandi was also divorced. Nobody really knew about their relationship. What's more, nobody knew that Sandi was pregnant.

One day, Sandi was trying to call Larry at home, but he wasn't answering his phone. She went to his house and found Larry dead. Police began investigating Larry's death and they suspected that Lloyd, Sandi's ex-husband, may have had something to do with the crime. The police believed Lloyd may have killed Larry in a jealous rage. Although the police arrested Lloyd and he went on trial for Larry's death, there wasn't enough evidence to prove the case against him, and he was released.

Eight months later, Lloyd remarried. And guess who his new wife was? Kathy, Larry's ex-wife! Police aren't sure when and how Lloyd and Kathy met. But since they were still convinced that Lloyd had something to do with Larry's death, they thought perhaps that Kathy had had something to do with it as well. The murder of Larry Sarvey is still unsolved. If Lloyd is guilty, we may never know, because he died in March 2009.

Larry Sarvey's house at 936 Price Boulevard was once the home of Joseph and Emma Haegelin. They both died inside the house. Beyond these deaths, however, the house on the hill is connected to several other strange and tragic endings. What is it about this address that has caused so much heartbreak?

When I went to visit the house, no one lived there because it was being renovated. As soon as I drove up, I felt a creepy energy. Even though I couldn't go inside to investigate, I used some ghost-hunting equipment outside and got some interesting results. My team and I set up our special ghost detectors in the yard, and what happened next gave us all goose bumps. Our equipment picked up a woman's presence standing right in the middle of the yard with two little girls beside her. She had other children around her as well—their

energy seemed very active, almost as if they were playing an invisible game of tag! This discovery made perfect sense. The Zibold family lived in the house next door, and since they were all relatives, the children probably ran back and forth between the houses, laughing and playing together. Most surprising of all, our ghost radio suddenly spelled out a name: *Emma*.

Who still walks the hallways inside that old house? Is Larry still sitting in his favorite chair, watching his ghostly television that only he can see? Is Emma still tucking her phantom children into beds that disappeared long ago? The next time you pass by this old house, look closely at the upstairs windows. That movement behind the curtain might not just be the wind . . .

CHAPTER 3

Ravenhearse Manor

This mansion is beautiful on the outside, and just as gorgeous on the inside. But what you'd never guess is that a mischievous little ghost girl is waiting in the shadows, eager to say hello to visitors brave enough to enter!

William Osborne, one of Atchison's wealthiest citizens, built this grand house for his daughter in 1884. When she grew up, she married the popular Mr. Parks, and the newlyweds made the mansion their home. Can you believe it only cost $26,462.60 to build back then? That's about what you'd pay for an average car today!

In 1894, this house became the center of the most talked-about scandal in town. Mr. and Mr. Parks had planned one of the grandest parties Atchison had ever seen. Everyone who was anyone in Atchison was excited to attend. But just days before the celebration, disaster struck—a dangerous smallpox outbreak swept through the town. Officials ordered everyone to stay home until the sickness passes, and all gatherings were forbidden.

Mr. Parks was furious! He had already spent a fortune on food and decorations—none of which could be returned. Refusing to cancel, he stormed into court on the morning of the party, but the judge firmly ordered him not to hold the celebration. Because it was too late to notify all the guests, police officers surrounded the manor at sunset, blocking the doorways and patrolling the grounds.

As darkness fell, the sound of piano music and dancing guests drifted through the windows. Whenever police approached the house, the music would suddenly stop and the house would fall eerily silent; but the moment officers walked away, the dancing and laughter would resume! Determined guests began scaling fences and sneaking through windows—some even disguised themselves to slip past the officers! By midnight, almost everyone had found their way inside. In a gesture of peace, the partygoers eventually brought bowls of ice cream out to the freezing police officers standing guard in the cold night air.

Another mysterious fact about this house: Abraham Lincoln once gave a speech beneath a massive oak tree that used to stand in the yard. (Some say you can still hear whispers of his words on quiet nights.)

Today, Bill Ravenhearse owns the mansion, living there with his partner and children. He's restoring the house to its former glory and offers spooky tours during the fall. Bill transforms himself into a vampire, complete with pale makeup and fangs, to tell chilling stories to wide-eyed visitors.

His son, Rocky, adored their spooky family tradition and loved sharing it with his father. Tragically, Rocky had an undiagnosed heart condition and passed away at just fifteen years old. To honor Rocky's memory, Bill continues the eerie performances that his son cherished. Rocky's spirit lives on not just in memory, but through the children whose lives were saved when his organs were donated after his death.

In addition to his family, Bill shares the mansion with an unusual pet—a glossy black raven named Marius who freely flies throughout the house and sleeps in a dog bed near Bill's room. Marius has become so popular with visitors that he even has his own social media account!

Since moving in, Bill has experienced countless unexplained events. He insists the ghosts are friendly, even if they do enjoy playing tricks on the living. During tours, visitors often notice the sudden, strong scent of baby powder floating through empty rooms. Sometimes, someone will feel a tug on their shirt, like a child trying to get their attention, when no one is there. Bill

has even heard the pitter-patter of small footsteps racing up and down the stairs in the middle of the night. The little ghost girl seems particularly fond of one antique dresser in the upstairs bedroom. She constantly removes the knobs and hides them around the house. Could there be a secret hidden in those drawers that she doesn't want anyone to discover?

If you're brave enough to meet this playful spirit, along with the other ghosts that wander these elegant halls, visit in the fall to hear one of Bill's spine-tingling tales. Just be prepared—the mansion's ghostly residents love surprising visitors when they least expect it!

CHAPTER 4

Halling-Fridell House

On the south side of Atchison, along the bluff of the Missouri River, stands a beautiful two-story home with a secret. This grand home was built by Mr. and Mrs. Blish in 1891, its windows overlooking the river below. The Blishes did not have any children, so when they passed away, they left their cherished home to their nephew, Wheeler Barlow.

In 1958, a dentist named Dr. Salvatore Scemica bought the house, making it his home until 1983. The property then passed to John Fridell and his wife, Mary Halling-Fridell, who lived there until 2020. Today, Anne and George Pruett own this historic residence—though they may not be the *only* ones who consider it home.

When my friend Tammy and I were researching haunted places in Atchison, we stopped by the house just hoping to take a picture from outside. To our surprise, George spotted us and excitedly invited us in for a tour. The moment we entered the house, Tammy froze. She was staring at something I couldn't see—a woman in an old-fashioned blue dress that looked to be from the early 1900s had appeared in the hallway! Tammy whispered that the woman seemed kind, but was curious about why we were there.

As we visited with George, he shared a chilling story that John Fridell had told him. One day, John was doing some woodworking down in the basement when he heard distinct footsteps creaking across the floor above his head. Assuming his wife, Mary, had come home from the store, he called out, "Mary, is that you?" But she did not answer.

He kept working, and about thirty minutes later, he again heard footsteps pacing overhead. Once more he called to her, "Mary, is that you?" This time, his wife's voice answered. When John came upstairs, he asked why she hadn't responded the first time. Mary looked puzzled and explained that she had just walked

in the door moments ago. Who, then, had been walking through their empty house?!

The couple also talked about their delicate glass figurines that sat on the mantel above the fireplace in the dining room. One day, they came home to find that every single figurine had been carefully moved from the dining room to the living room. Nothing was broken—just moved, as if someone had decided to redecorate while they were away.

Once, I was lucky enough to stay overnight in the house with some friends, who also happened to be fellow ghost hunters. Using our specialized paranormal equipment, we were able to communicate with the woman in the blue dress, as well as a male presence we detected upstairs. Our devices would light up in response to specific questions, as if invisible fingers were touching them. Most incredibly, our audio recorder captured a woman's soft voice that none of us had heard during the session. We believe the woman in blue is Mrs. Blish herself, still watching over the home she loved so much. The male presence upstairs seems to be Mr. Barlow, perhaps checking in on his aunt's property.

Thanks to George and Anne, you can experience these paranormal encounters for yourself! They've converted the historic home into a vacation rental where brave guests can spend the night. If you come for a visit, remember your manners—be sure to say hello to Mrs. Blish and thank her for allowing you to stay in her home. After all, it's only polite to thank your host . . . even if she's been dead for over a century!

CHAPTER 5

Dilgert House

The house at 919 Atchison Street holds secrets as solid as its foundation. Built in 1880 by a German immigrant named Adam Dilgert, the home's walls have witnessed both family life and terrible tragedy. Adam lived there with his wife and three children, establishing himself as an important figure in Atchison for two very different reasons.

Adam's limestone quarry supplied the sturdy material for countless home foundations throughout Atchison, quite literally helping to build the growing town. But Adam was equally known for his frightening temper that flared dangerously whenever he drank.

One fateful night, Adam and his construction crew were at the Zibold-Haegelin brewery celebrating the completion of a construction job. Adam's brother Ferdinand was also there, nursing his own mug of beer at a nearby table. Adam and his brother didn't always get along, and as the night wore on and the alcohol flowed freely, harsh words were exchanged. Their argument escalated until Adam's fist flew into Ferdinand's face with a powerful punch, sending his brother sprawling.

Ferdinand staggered home dazed and disoriented. Hours later, he was found dead in his bed. Adam stood trial for his brother's death, but without enough evidence to prove it, Adam walked free. (Whether or not he ever escaped the guilt of what happened that night is another story.)

In 2014, a woman named Keli Adams purchased the old Dilgert house, excited to restore its historic beauty. But her renovation plans quickly hit unexpected obstacles. Construction workers frequently abandoned their work before finishing, refusing to return. Some reported hearing heavy footsteps following them through empty room. Others glimpsed shadowy figures watching them from doorways. One terrified worker discovered a horrifying sight in the basement—a dead blackbird with its eyes gouged out, arranged like some kind of warning. He gathered his tools and left immediately, never to return.

During the renovations, Keli made a strange discovery: an old cavalry boot buried deep in the basement floor. Adam Dilgert had served in the Civil War, so Keli thought perhaps the boot might have belonged to him. Some Europeans have a tradition of burying shoes within a house to ward off evil spirits and protect the family. But if that was Adam's intention, it seemed the protection failed—because something, or *someone*, definitely lingers in the house.

My paranormal investigation teammates and I were able to tour the home with our ghost hunting equipment. Our K2 meter, which detects electromagnetic movement, went off several times. And when using our ghost box, the voice of a very stern-sounding woman speaking German came through. We believe this had to be Adam's wife, Mrs. Dilgert herself,

still watching over her home—and perhaps her troubled husband.

Today, the home is owned by Camille and her husband, who have continued to restore it while uncovering its mysterious past. Camille regularly hears unexplained footsteps and glimpses shadows darting around corners. She believes a young boy's spirit plays in the basement; perhaps one of the Dilgert children or another child from the house's long history. Camille welcomes curious visitors to tour her home and—if they're feeling extra brave—try to communicate with the spirits that never left. Many guests have reported cold spots, whispering voices, and the eerie feeling of being watched in otherwise empty rooms.

If you find yourself in Atchison with courage to spare, stop by the Dilgert House. But be warned: you may meet more than one resident from its troubled past!

CHAPTER 6

Glick Mansion

This gorgeous house sits directly across the street from the infamous Sallie House! For seventy-one years, it was home to the George Glick family. George and his wife, Lizzie, liked adding onto the house, so it was under construction for decades after it was built. George was very well-known in town. He loved to farm and owned lots of land in Atchison. Eventually, he became a lawyer and then the

Governor of Kansas. If you visit the US Capitol Building in Washington, D.C., you can find a statue of George standing proudly in Statuary Hall.

When George and Lizzie's daughter, Jennie, married James Orr, the newlyweds decided to live in the mansion with her parents. Soon, Jennie and James had a son whom they named George after his famous grandfather.

Years later, in a series of hard times, the family would tragically lose George to an accident at the beach. This was a terrible blow to the governor and his wife, because George was their only grandson and had grown up living with them in the mansion. George was twenty-five and had just gotten married. The couple even had a new home waiting for them to return from their honeymoon, full of wedding gifts they hadn't yet opened. During their honeymoon at La Jolla Beach in San

Diego, California, George was relaxing on the beach with his new bride when a strong wave came and suddenly swept him out to sea. He was never seen alive again.

After Jennie and her husband, James, passed away, there was no family left to inherit the historic home. In 1992, Ray and Joyce Barmby purchased the mansion and turned it into a bed and breakfast. (A bed and breakfast is similar to a hotel, but feels more like you are a guest in someone's cozy home.)

Though the Tuck U Inn closed down in 2022, former guests often reported hearing footsteps in empty hallways and doors that would open and close by themselves. Some awoke to find a full-body apparition standing over them—close enough to see all its features—only to vanish when they sat up! Could it have been George or Lizzie Glick, still watching over the home they loved so dearly? Or, might young

George's spirit have returned to the place where he grew up, forever frozen in time?

Once, when my friend Tammy and I drove by, we could still feel the ghostly energy just outside the house. Tammy sensed the presence of a woman who seemed to miss the former owners of the bed and breakfast, because they'd always set out fresh flowers that smelled so nice. Tammy also thought the ghost didn't like how quiet the house had become now that guests no longer came to stay.

Hopefully, the new owners love the house as much as Mr. and Mrs. Glick, and Mr. and Mrs. Barmby, and make the ghosts feel welcome too. Maybe even occasionally, they will set out fresh flowers for Mrs. Lizzie.

CHAPTER 7

McInteer Villa

One of the most beautiful houses in Atchison is also very, very (did I say very?), *very* haunted! This grand Victorian house at 1301 Kansas Avenue is known as the McInteer Villa. John McInteer, a very successful saddle maker in Atchison, built the house in 1889 for his family. The house was his way of showing Atchison just how successful he was.

My paranormal investigative team and I have stayed in the home several times, once for as long as a week. Incredibly, nine people have died in the McInteer Villa, most of them former owners of the house who died while they were home. Sometimes, the ghosts seem only to want to say hello before moving on. So, when you tour this beautiful home, you never know which spirit you might encounter.

Up until 1925, the house was owned and occupied by the McInteers and members of their extended family. It then became a boarding house until 1952, when Isobel "Goldie" Altus bought the house and moved to Atchison from Washington, D.C., where she'd worked for the FBI.

Because Goldie lived in the large house alone and frequently dressed in black, her neighbors whispered that she was strange, or "eccentric." Kids in the neighborhood went even further—they called her a witch and vandalized her property. Goldie often sat in her rocking chair watching the neighborhood from the window of her front room. Not feeling safe, she kept a loaded gun in her lap. In fact, when Goldie died, they found her still sitting in that *same* rocking chair in her front room, as if still keeping watch. This is often where the ghost of Goldie is still seen, heard, and felt. Her actual rocking chair remains in that room, and sometimes visitors touring the house swear they can see it moving all by itself!

The residents who lived in the house after Goldie were the Gerardys. Mr. and Mrs. Gerardy lived in the home for decades, raising their children there, and later welcoming grandchildren who played in the same rooms. Mrs. Gerardy told the *Kansas City Star* that she had a few ghostly experiences in the house. She had seen a strange shadow lurking near her children's bedroom, a woman in a white dress, a boy, and a woman in a pink dress.

Today, Stephanie O'Reilly owns the house and welcomes brave visitors who want to meet its ghostly residents. She has seen the ghost of Mr. Gerardy on the front porch in his overalls, just as he did in life, and has experienced countless other unexplained events. Lights flicker off and on by themselves, eerie voices whisper, balls bounce down the stairs in the middle of the night—as if someone or *something* has kicked them—and doors swing open and slam shut all on their own. It seems no room is safe from the ghostly mischief . . . after all, it happens in every room and every corner of the house!

When my paranormal team and I visited, a man's loud whistling followed us down the stairs, though we couldn't see anyone there! Something kept knocking over one of our cameras—three times in just a couple of days. Strangely, none of our other cameras were touched. (Perhaps some of the ghosts were more camera-shy than others?)

If you're feeling brave, take a tour with Stephanie and listen to her wild stories about the house. But beware . . . they are real!

CHAPTER 8

Hannah Jo Cusack

Hannah Jo Cusack and J.K. Cusack were married in 1861. But sadly, J.K. passed away just five years after their wedding, and Hannah never remarried. She moved to Atchison after her husband's death and lived at 1009 Parallel Street—and some say she never left!

Hannah was a milliner, a person who makes or sells hats, particularly women's hats. Impressively, Hannah became famous all over the world for her hats trimmed with painted cornhusks. She won awards, was featured in national magazines, and even sold her hats to famous people like Queen Victoria.

The current residents, Sharon and Max Berry, moved into the home in 2005. They loved the history of the house, and Sharon hoped that Hannah would still be there.

"Once I walked in," Sharon said, "I got the feeling I was home and never wanted to leave." When the Berrys began remodeling the house, Sharon started talking to Hannah. She would ask Hannah which paint color she preferred. The next morning, she would awake to find a penny left on a paint can, as if Hannah had chosen her favorite color.

Soon, pennies became a trend around the house. Max found a penny inside a chandelier that hung from an eleven-foot-high ceiling, and a workman found a penny inside a toilet tank. Pennies continued to be found in odd places where it was unlikely someone could have hidden them. Each time they found a new penny, Sharon and Max put the coin in a box and thanked Hannah for "speaking" to them.

Intrigued by all the strange happenings, Sharon invited a psychic and paranormal investigation team over to investigate. During their visit, the team made contact with a child ghost who insisted on being called Katie. The psychic also saw a woman tending to a garden whom she felt strongly was Hannah, still caring for the property she'd loved so deeply in life.

Sharon's experiences weren't limited to human spirits. Countless times, she'd felt something soft and furry brushing against her legs, even though her own cat was nowhere nearby. Sometimes, late at night, distinct meows

would echo, as if phantom felines still patrolled the hallways they once called home.

It seems Sharon finally got her wish to live in a haunted house—maybe *more* haunted than she ever imagined! If you drive by the Hannah Jo Cusack home on a quiet evening, look carefully. You might just see Hannah waving from the upstairs window or tending to garden flowers that only she can see.

Part Two

Creeptastic Culture

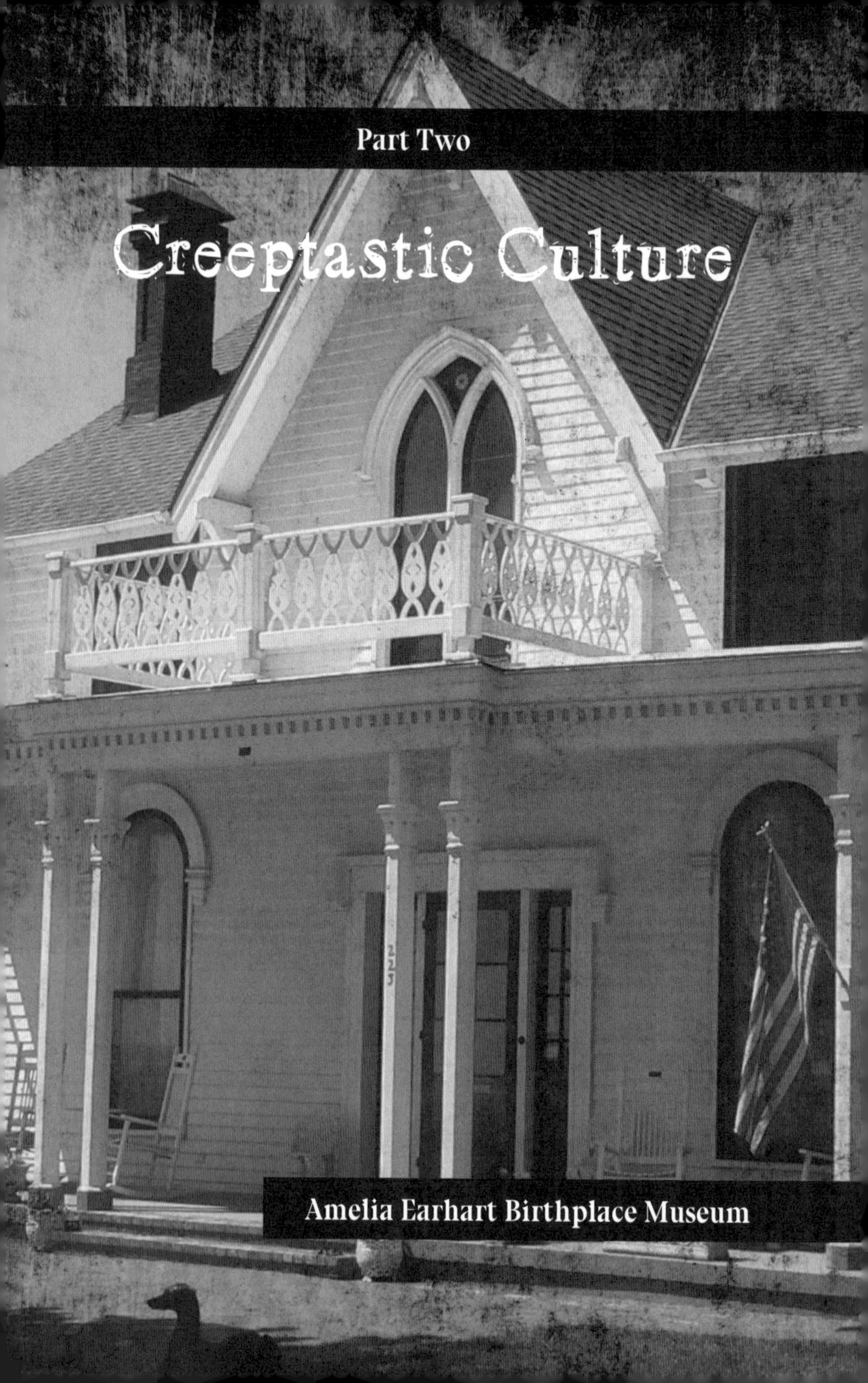

Amelia Earhart Birthplace Museum

CHAPTER 9

Amelia Earhart Birthplace Museum

In the early 1900s, there was a little girl named Amelia who lived in Atchison. Her parents gave her the nickname "Meeley" and her younger sister, Muriel, went by "Pidge." Meeley and Pidge loved playing together. They explored every inch of their neighborhood—climbing the tallest trees they could find and hunting rats in old barns.

Amelia wasn't like other girls of her time. Rather than wearing dresses, Amelia liked to wear pants (better for climbing and exploring), and her mother allowed her to dress differently. She also loved taking risks—something that would continue to be a passion of hers even as she became an adult. Once, Amelia and her uncle built a wooden ramp off the shed roof. As she zoomed down the ramp in a wooden box, she exclaimed, "Look! I'm flying!" Little did anyone know that Amelia's love of flying and adventure would only continue to inspire her.

This fearless little girl from Atchison grew up to become none other than the legendary Amelia Earhart—the first woman to fly a plane solo across the Atlantic Ocean, in 1932! Being a female aviator, or pilot, was nearly unheard of in those days, but Amelia never cared much about what others thought was "proper" for women and young ladies.

On July 2, 1937, Amelia's plane mysteriously vanished as she attempted to become the first woman to fly solo around the entire world. Although she was officially declared dead in 1939, her disappearance remains one of history's greatest unsolved mysteries. No one knows what truly happened to Amelia Earhart and her plane.

Today, the house where Amelia was born is now a museum to celebrate and honor this trailblazing woman and her incredible achievements. Visitors can learn about her life as a child and her accomplishments as a woman aviator. You can see the bedroom

where she slept as a little girl and her personal dresser, which Amelia's grandmother had made especially for her with "Amelia 1904" burned into the wood. But there's even more to this house than meets the eye . . . because some say Amelia's adventurous spirit never left this place at all.

Museum employees have heard footsteps on the stairs when nobody else is in the house. One night, the museum caretaker was working alone when all the lights suddenly turned on by themselves! Other employees have seen unexplained flashes of light darting through darkened hallways.

When I visited the museum with my ghost-hunting team and asked a question about Amelia, something invisible touched a piece of our equipment. Could it have been Amelia herself, reaching out to let us know she was listening?

Sometimes you can feel ghosts, even though you can't see them. Visitors will report sudden goosebumps or tingling skin in certain rooms—especially Amelia's bedroom.

Perhaps Amelia's adventurous spirt still soars through her childhood home, watching over her legacy and making sure her incredible story continues to inspire a new generation of dreamers.

The museum welcomes visitors daily. If you do get a chance to visit, pay special attention when you enter Amelia's bedroom. Those sudden *chills* running down your spine? That might just be Amelia herself, checking to see if you share her great love of adventure!

CHAPTER 10

Theatre Atchison

After Atchison was founded, several buildings served as theaters in the growing city. But for one reason or another, none of these structures became a permanent home for the city's arts and entertainment. Today, the Theatre Atchison is housed in what was originally the Christian Science Church, built in 1914. The theater organization was established in 1948 and continues to put on wonderful plays, including several children's shows each year.

Not long ago, my friend Tammy and I met with Travis Grossman, the executive director who has worked at the theater for over twenty years. Boy, did he have some ghost stories to share! When we first sat down with Travis in his office, Tammy suddenly went quiet. She pointed to the top of the stairs and whispered that she could see a woman in a maroon dress standing there. Travis said, "That's interesting because I hear footsteps on these stairs all the time, and it sounds like someone is walking around at the top of the stairs." He explained that it often sounds as if a person is stepping off the stairs into the locked second-floor lobby area. Since that area is always secured, there's no way a person, or at least a *living* person, could be making those sounds.

Travis also said that many guests have heard mysterious voices echoing through empty rooms. Even more intriguing, children performing in plays at the theater have told him that they have seen and heard the ghosts, including the ghost of a headless man!

Once, a technician working in the theater late at night found himself completely alone in the big, dark theater when he started hearing strange noises and whispering voices coming from the attic. He thought maybe someone had gotten inside and was hiding in the attic. But when he went to check, nobody was there.

Another employee named Charles was alone in the theater one night. He had just turned off all the lights to go home when a loud voice shouted, "Hey!"—as if to tell Charles to turn the light back on. He did, thinking someone was still in the theater with him, but nobody was there.

On Halloween night, Charles was again alone in the theater. Suddenly, he heard the locked front doors begin to rattle, as if someone was trying to get inside. Thinking neighborhood kids were playing pranks, he decided to ignore it. But then it happened again, even more forcefully. This time, he ran to the entrance and yanked the doors open, certain he'd catch the pranksters in the act. Imagine his confusion—and alarm—when he found only empty darkness outside. It didn't make any sense. Charles was sure he'd heard someone trying to get inside, hadn't he? An eerie feeling swept over him. Unless . . . could something *inside* the theater have been trying to get OUT? Something . . . not of this world?

The next time you visit the Theatre Atchison for a show, make sure to enjoy the amazing performances and appreciate all the hard work that goes into making the theater magic happen. Just don't be surprised if you realize the person sitting next to you . . . isn't really there at all.

CHAPTER 11

Cray Historical Home Museum

The Evah Cray Historical Home Museum is another jaw-dropping example of Atchison's beautiful Victorian architecture. The home and carriage house were built in 1882, by W. W. Hetherington, the son of the founder of the Exchange Bank of Atchison. A well-known resident of the city, his nickname was "the Atchison Millionaire." This stunning home, which is painted white, has two three-story towers that were inspired by Mrs. Hetherington's love for Scottish castles. The house has twenty-five rooms, five beautiful fireplaces, ornately carved woodwork, and original chandeliers on the first floor.

The Hetherington family and their descendants lived in the home for eighty years. After changing hands several times over the decades, Cloud and Evah Cray eventually bought the home in 1978. Evah loved to collect antiques, and the house was the perfect place for her to display her extensive collection.

Today, this historic home serves as a fascinating museum. The carriage house has been converted to a gift shop, a small theater where visitors can watch a short film about the house and its rich history, and the director's office. But maybe most notably, the carriage house also seems to have acquired some spectral residents!

When it was being remodeled, the museum installed a new projector to show the film about the history of the house. That's when the mysterious problems began. Despite being brand new, the projector quit working. The frustrated staff tried to figure out what was wrong, but had no luck. The problem with the projector only stopped after the staff moved several of Evah Cray's most prized antiques from the carriage house into a room in one of the home's towers.

It was almost as if Mrs. Cray herself was sending a message from beyond the grave—urging the staff to take better care of her belongings. She wanted them safe inside her beloved home, *not* in the carriage house. Even in death, it seems Evah Cray still guards her prized collection, making sure each antique receives the loving care and attention it deserves.

CHAPTER 12

Santa Fe Depot

The Santa Fe Depot building is one of the first things you might see driving into Atchison. While its impressive exterior looks like it did when it was built in 1880, the interior has taken on a new look for the residents of Atchison to enjoy. Today, the historical building houses the Chamber of Commerce, the Atchison Historical Society, the Atchison Visitors Center, and the Atchison County Historical Museum. It's also the home of the world's smallest "unofficial" presidential library.

David Atchison, whom the city is named after, served as a Missouri senator from 1843 to 1855. When Zachary Taylor refused to be sworn in as President on March 4, 1849 because it was a Sunday, something strange happened. Some people claim that David Atchison (who was filling in as Senate president) accidentally became the President of the United States for just one day—until Taylor took over on Monday! This would have been the shortest presidency ever. Historians agree this story isn't really true, but it's still a fun piece of Atchison history.

When the railroads arrived in Atchison in the early 1870s, getting goods to the city became easier. The railroads also made traveling easier, as trains were able to transport many more people than stagecoaches. But with the progress and prosperity the railroads brought to Atchison also came some darker tales—stories that still haunt the city today.

One summer night in 1882, a train engineer named Britt Craft was driving his train near Cawker City, a town about two hundred miles west of Atchison. As the train roared along the tracks, Britt suddenly noticed something terrifying ahead: a bridge they were about to cross was engulfed in flames! He had to act

quickly. Instead of continuing over the burning bridge, he slammed on the train's brakes. The train derailed and tumbled into the creek below. Britt was thrown from the locomotive and died that night, but his actions and quick thinking saved the lives of every passenger on board.

In the Mount Vernon Cemetery, a seven-foot-tall stone memorial of a train honors Britt Craft. But some say his spirit never left the tracks where he met his tragic end. When the bridge was rebuilt, the first passenger train to cross the new bridge reported something chilling. As they passed the location of the accident, the conductor suddenly heard the whistling of a train. When he leaned out the window to investigate, he saw a ghostly white figure that looked like Britt Craft standing along the tracks!

The shaken conductor told his story to anyone who would listen. For years afterward, crews reported a similar sight: a ghostly man standing near the rebuilt bridge watching trains pass . . . perhaps to keep them safe? Some visitors to the Santa Fe Depot say they can still hear the distant sound of a steam whistle, even when no trains are running.

Another railroad worker whose restless spirit still haunts the Santa Fe Depot building was Bill "Hangman" Fields, a fearless and dedicated man with an unusual talent. Bill earned his nickname from his daring method of hanging onto freight as it was hoisted into train cars. Passersby would often spot Bill dangling happily high above the railway, waving to them as he swung through the air.

But one fateful day, tragedy struck. While Bill was working with a particularly heavy load of freight, the rope he was hanging from snapped—sending Bill plummeting to his death. Today, some museum visitors report the sound of footsteps in a part of the building no longer in use. Many people believe it's Bill, still cheerfully doing the job he loved so much and unaware that his life has ended.

With so many historical treasures at the Santa Fe Depot, it's no wonder that visitors report frequent paranormal experiences. Museums often hold items of such meaning and importance to their original owners that those spirits simply can't bear to part with them, even in death. Some ghost

hunters believe that cherished objects never lose their energy from the past. So if you ever hear or see something unexplained while wandering through the depot building, don't fear. It's probably just a friendly spirit, like Bill "Hangman" Fields, returning for a visit.

Part Three

Eerie Eateries

CHAPTER 13

Riverhouse Restaurant

The building at 101 Commercial Street is one of the oldest in Atchison. In the city's early days, the location served as the headquarters of the Atchison & Nebraska Railroad, a hotel, a firehouse, and the meeting place of the Rotary Club of Atchison.

It has been home to several different restaurants, and many who have had the pleasure of eating there have discovered that ghostly experiences are on the menu.

One Halloween season in 2007, a guest was eating at the restaurant. Having heard the stories, they asked their server, "Are there really ghosts in this place?"

"Yes!" the server answered. "There is a female ghost that likes to hang out in the ladies' restroom. I have never seen the ghost before, but I have seen a mirror fly off the wall and break. I have also seen a person's cell phone fly off a table and soar across the room."

One customer was dining at the restaurant for her birthday and went upstairs to use the bathroom. While washing her hands, she felt like someone was with her, although the bathroom was empty. When she looked in the mirror, she saw the face of a woman behind her.

Former managers have described seeing lights turn off by themselves. They also made sure to steer clear of the basement, which they said gave them the creeps. The lightbulb on the basement stairs broke many times for no apparent reason and often had to be replaced. Workers also sometimes heard footsteps going up and down the stairs when nobody was there.

While I was in Atchison collecting stories, I spoke to a woman named Geneeka, who used to be a waitress at this restaurant. I asked Geneeka, "Have you ever had any *experiences*?" Her eyes opened wide, and she replied, "Oh yes! That place is very haunted!" She described seeing the ghostly image of a woman on the back patio one night after her shift was over. She had also heard the same spooky footsteps in the basement, and seen pictures that customers took at the restaurant showing a spectral, ghostlike person.

Though the Riverhouse Restaurant has now permanently closed its doors, one can't help but wonder if its ghostly residents have moved on too. Perhaps they still wander the old dining room, eternally tied to a place where laughter and festivity remain.

CHAPTER 14

Paolucci's Deli

Not only can you get some of the best chicken fingers at Paolucci's, you might also eat lunch with a ghost! The deli was opened in 1894 by Rosa and Dominic Paolucci, and their family still owns the business today. First, the location was a grocery store and the Paolucci family lived above the store. Eventually, the upstairs was turned into a hotel named the Old

Traveler's Hotel. Today, the downstairs is the deli and a restaurant, and upstairs is a bar.

I spoke to Margie, the current owner. She told me stories of her family and gave me a tour of the restaurant. I could feel how proud Margie was of her family's business as she told her stories.

A few paranormal investigation teams have visited the restaurant looking to speak to a ghost—and have succeeded! One team told Margie that they sensed two male ghosts upstairs. They thought those men were named Nick and John, sons of Rosa and Dominic Paolucci. Some former employees have also reported eerie experiences. One bartender said she was cleaning up one night after all the customers had gone home. She heard voices, like people talking, even though she was alone.

Other workers have seen a ghostly image of a man appear before them—only to disappear a moment later.

One waitress shared something truly spine-tingling with me—that she sometimes hears a woman's voice calling her name. But when she turns around and asks who's calling her, her coworkers just stare like they have no idea what she's talking about. On another occasion, a boy went into the bathroom, only to run out frightened a moment later. When I asked him what had happened, he said the sink faucet had suddenly turned on all by itself. This story made me smile. Perhaps the female spirit—maybe Rosa Paolucci herself?—was just trying to remind the boy to wash his hands.

CHAPTER 15

Lopez de Mexico

If you like chips, salsa, tacos—*and* ghosts!—Lopez de Mexico is the place to go. Located in downtown Atchison, this family-owned restaurant will not disappoint. The restaurant's story began with Enrique Lopez, who emigrated from Mexico at age eight. He married Elena Vallejo, who was born in Horton, Kansas—a town nicknamed "Little Mexico" because of its large Mexican population who came to work for the Rock Island Railroad. In Atchison, they became known as Helen and Henry. In 1995, the couple opened Lopez de Mexico to share their culture through food and music. Their motto of treating customers "like part of the family" continues today, as the restaurant remains within the Lopez-Vallejo family. Many employees have worked there since it first opened.

The first time I went, I was interested in more than just the salsa. I asked for Anne, the manager. When she came over, I introduced myself and asked her, "Do you ever have things happen here you can't explain?" She smiled and said she would be back to tell me some stories after I finished my meal. Her stories were the perfect dessert.

The story Anne shared with me was about a woman in a black dress. One year, a psychic was in town visiting for the fall festivities. She was eating in the restaurant and asked Anne, "Who is the lady in the black dress?" but Anne didn't see anyone. "She has dark hair pulled into a bun and a long black dress with tall black boots," the psychic continued. "She looks upset at her waitress with the red hair." The psychic pointed to the waitress she was talking about.

Anne's eyes widened in shock. She had just spoken to that waitress because of an upset customer. Apparently, the lady in the black dress was not happy with the waitress either!

Another time, Annie's husband, George—who was a bit of a skeptic when it came to ghosts—overheard a customer describing the very same woman in the black dress. His ears perked up immediately and he decided to ask the customer some questions. When the man perfectly described the woman's dress and boots, and the way she'd followed the waitstaff around telling them what to do—"Hurry up, clean these tables!"—George was shocked. Maybe the ghostly woman *was* real?

Though nobody knows exactly who the lady in the black dress might have been in life, it seems she takes great pride in the restaurant. So if you ever visit Lopez de Mexico and feel someone watching you, or notice the hair on the back of your neck suddenly stand up as you pass the kitchen, just offer a polite nod to the lady in black. After all, she's just making sure you get the best service possible!

CHAPTER 16

Pete's Steakhouse

Another spooky downtown treasure is Pete's Steakhouse. Revekkah, the owner, serves up some delicious dishes inspired by her Greek heritage. Her family came to America from Greece, bringing their rich culinary traditions that now delight Atchison diners.

When I asked my server if they'd experienced anything unusual, she sent

Revekkah right to our table. Revekkah was a bit skeptical. "I am too busy running around here working to notice anything," she told me. "But, I do have an employee with some interesting stories!"

Revekkah introduced him and he showed us the basement, which the restaurant uses as storage. The basement may have been a bar or speakeasy during the Prohibition era, when drinking and selling alcohol was illegal. As we followed the man down the creaky basement stairs, my team and I felt the presence of a male spirit. The employee told us that he

has, in fact, seen a ghostly man down in the basement. But that's not all—he has also seen two women who look like they are talking to each other. He said that whenever he comes downstairs, the spectral women stop talking and stare. Even stranger? He gets the feeling the ghostly man and women don't interact, as if they want nothing to do with each other.

Other employees have their own stories. They say the light upstairs turns off and on by itself. Sometimes voices can be heard when the

restaurant has no customers. Many customers have told Revekkah that they've heard or seen things they cannot explain. Perhaps, after all this time and so many encounters, Revekkah is starting to wonder . . . could there be truth to some of these stories?

If you're in Atchison—and in the mood for something truly *out of this world*—make sure you visit Pete's. Just know you may have some unexpected guests join your party!

CHAPTER 17

Zibold-Haegelin Brewery

When pioneers were moving west and settling in Atchison, one popular place for the local residents to gather was the Zibold-Haegelin Brewery. The brewery is named after the two men who owned it, Herman Zibold and Josef Haegelin. Herman and Josef immigrated to America from Germany. Joseph first moved to St. Joseph, Missouri. There he worked for a man who taught him how to brew beer, and became an experienced maltster. (A maltster is the person who selects the grain that is used to make the malt, one of the main ingredients in beer.) That brewery is where Joseph and Herman met, and when they moved to Atchison, they decided to combine their skills and start a business together. Joseph also fell in love with and married Herman's sister, Emma, so now they were business partners and brothers-in-law!

Joseph and Emma loved Atchison. The city reminded them of the town they left in Germany. Joseph and Herman built the large brewery, which eventually consisted of seven buildings. They also built homes for the families across the street. The location of the brewery and houses was near Tenth Street and Price Boulevard. The residents of Atchison would go to the brewery to hear bands play, dance, and spend time together. If someone was throwing a large party, they often used the brewery as a place to gather. Eventually, an ice-skating rink was added, and groups of people would come after church on Sundays.

But not everyone liked having breweries in Atchison—or in the state of Kansas. There was a group of people who were pushing to pass prohibition laws, which would ban anyone from buying or selling any kind of alcohol. Eventually, in 1879, Kansas became a "dry state." This was what they called a state that passed the prohibition laws. People didn't want to break the law, so they stopped coming to the brewery. It became difficult for Joseph

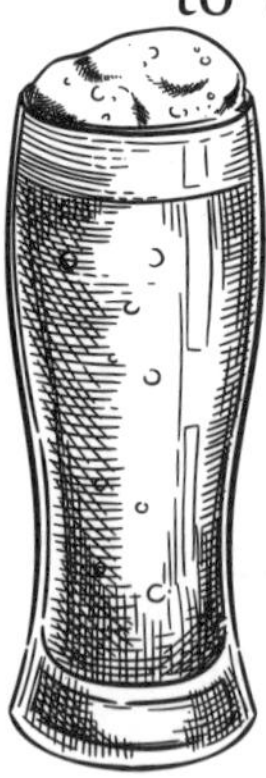

and Herman to keep their once-thriving business open. Herman decided to fight the prohibition law and took his case all the way to the US Supreme Court. Although this made the brewery nationally famous, Herman did not win. The court agreed with the State of Kansas and upheld the law.

Not everyone wanted to follow the new law, though, including Sheriff J.A. Martin, whose job it was to enforce the law. The sheriff would arrest Joseph or Herman, but instead of taking them to jail, they would spend time at the sheriff's house. He was doing this to make it look like he was enforcing the laws, even though he wasn't.

Today, a park sits on the land where the brewery once operated. The houses are still standing but the brewery is no longer there. Still, if you listen closely, you might just hear echoes from the past. As you stroll through the park, listen for music from a faraway band playing, the clinking of beer mugs, and the sounds of laughter, whispering through the trees. The brewery may be gone, but don't tell that to the ghostly residents of Atchison. . . .

Part Four

The Otherworldly Outdoors

CHAPTER 18

Missouri River

The beautiful Missouri River flows with a swift, strong current. The river has its own folklore or legends, and despite its beauty, also holds some dark secrets.

One of these tales is about a young woman who was riding her buggy down Atchison Street near the ferry entrance one winter night. This part of the street that heads toward the river is very steep, and that night it was also icy. At the bottom of the hill sat the entrance to the ferry, where people could get on and ride to the other side of the river.

Unfortunately, on the way down the hill, the young woman's horses started to slip on the icy street. She lost control of her buggy, and the horses skidded all the way toward the water, plunging into the river with the woman still onboard. The current quickly carried her down the river and she was never seen again.

Many people claim that if you walk along the river, especially at night, you can hear the woman call for them to join her in the river.

Some say they've seen a misty figure standing at the water's edge, extending a pale hand toward passersby before disappearing into the mist. Perhaps she's still searching for someone to help her find her way home—or maybe she's looking for company in her watery grave. Just remember, should you ever find yourself walking along the Missouri River after dark and happen to hear a woman's voice whispering your name . . . don't answer!

CHAPTER 19

Jackson Park

If you live in Atchison, you have probably spent some time at Jackson Park. Here, you can enjoy a walk along the paths, a picnic, disc golf, or birdwatching. When it was first established, the park was just known as "City Park." In the early 1900s, a well-known resident named Zaremba E. Jackson pushed to expand the park and it was renamed in his honor. Today, Jackson Park covers more than one hundred acres of land. But despite its beautiful setting, when night falls, everything changes—the park becomes a spooky place where shadows seem to move on their own and eerie whispers echo through the trees.

Many locations within the park are connected to local legends or folklore. These stories have been told for decades, but they are impossible to prove—*or* disprove. One of the legends is about a local teenage girl named Molly. Molly is said to have been out with her boyfriend on prom night. After prom, the couple went to the park. They got into a fight and Molly's boyfriend became so angry that he killed her. Another version of the story goes that after their fight, Molly's boyfriend left her in the park. She was so sad and upset that she took her own life.

For years, many people claim that they have seen Molly's ghost walking sadly among the trees. Others say that Molly has touched them, grabbing and tugging at their clothes. I drove the winding road that leads toward a hill overlooking the Missouri River. I had no idea at the time where the road went. I was using a word generator app that gives me word answers to my questions. The path was dark and windy, and I was unsure of where it was heading. I asked, "Should I keep going or turn around?" The equipment said, "decide

now." Was that a warning to turn around, or an encouragement to keep driving? I wasn't sure how to turn around safely on the narrow road, so I kept going. I am glad I did because the view from the overlook was gorgeous.

Make sure you visit Jackson Park during your time in Atchison. Spend some time playing, walking, and hiking with family and friends—or bring your binoculars to spot unique birds hanging out in the trees. Just be aware that when the sun goes down and evening shadows grow long, you might encounter . . . a *different* kind of visitor.

If you feel someone gently tap your shoulder and turn to find no one there, don't be alarmed. It's probably just Molly, coming to say hello. Perhaps she's hoping to find someone who'll listen to her side of the story after all these years. Will it be you?

CHAPTER 20

Cemeteries of Atchison

There are many reasons why Atchison is haunted, but the troubled history of its dead is definitely one of the spookiest. Early pioneers settling in the area or passing through faced deadly diseases like Spanish flu, cholera, smallpox, and tuberculosis. These illnesses spread quickly, claiming victims of all ages. Some families lost multiple members to diseases with no cure, leading to lives filled with grief, loss, and unfinished business.

Before Atchison existed as a town, the Kansa tribe lived along the riverside. Their burial rituals were led by tribal women who painted the deceased's face, wrapped the body in buffalo skin, and gave the spirit directions to the "land of the dead." They buried their dead on hillsides in shallow graves with pipes, food, and weapons.

The earliest documented grave in Atchison was discovered near Division Street Public School when construction workers unearthed Native American bones with spears and arrowheads. This site was close to the Sallie House and likely near the first Indigenous settlements on elevated land.

Shortly after, smallpox devastated Mormon settlers in the 1840s. Workers later discovered their bones while digging cellars for homes or creating streets. Settlers buried other Mormon dead near West Atchison off Military Street, where years of farming eventually destroyed their graves.

No one knows what happened to these bones after they were dug up. Many believe the

constant disturbance of graves, the disrespect shown to the dead, and the forgotten remains of those who were forced away may explain why restless spirits still haunt Atchison.

Today, you can view the first Atchison cemetery at the Evah Cray Museum. Here, a single, weathered grave marker stands as

the last remnant of the town's original 1856 cemetery. As Atchison expanded, graves were relocated to an area called Block 56. But history soon repeated itself when this second graveyard—and the bodies buried inside—had to be moved due to the town's growth.

Unfortunately, some of the dead had no living relatives to pay for another relocation. While some bodies were moved to Oak Hill Cemetery, over one hundred souls were simply abandoned and forgotten in Block 56. Their graves were eventually paved over, erased from Atchison's memory. Later, homes would be built right on top of the unmarked graves.

Perhaps this explains the mysterious phenomena that some of the residents in those homes still report today. They hear footsteps creaking in empty rooms, see doors open and close by themselves, and hear voices whispering even when nobody else is around. Could it be the forgotten dead making themselves known? As if to remind people that they were here, too?

Oak Hill Cemetery served as Atchison's main burial ground until 1864, when Mount Vernon Cemetery was established. Wealthy families often transferred their deceased loved ones to this newer, more respectable location.

But headstones and flowers aren't the *only* things visitors encounter as these historic cemeteries.

Neighbors living near Oak Hill frequently report eerie activity after dark—shadowy figures moving between graves and strange lights hovering above tombstones. Thinking mischievous teenagers are trespassing, they'll call the police, who arrive only to find nobody in the cemetery. (Nobody *alive*, that is.)

Mount Vernon Cemetery has a section known locally as "Whisper Alley." Visitors

walking this path report hearing faint, ghostly murmurs that seem to follow them, only to grow louder when they try to leave. Near the cemetery's first pine tree, several visitors have even come face-to-face with a full-bodied apparition that vanishes as suddenly as it appears. It seems in Atchison, the line between the living and the dead is blurred. After all, when a town is built upon disturbed graves, can anyone truly ever rest in peace?

A Ghostly Goodbye

Atchison isn't just a dot on the map of Kansas—it's a place where the past refuses to stay buried. From the whispers in Mount Vernon Cemetery to the playful spirits of the Sallie House, the ghostly residents of this river town have plenty of stories to tell if you're brave enough to listen.

The next time you visit Atchison, keep your eyes open and your senses alert. That cold spot you feel while touring a historic mansion? The footsteps following you up a staircase when no one's there? The rocking chair moving on its own in an empty room? These might just be Atchison's permanent residents saying hello from the other side.

Whether you believe in ghosts or not, these stories connect us to the people who came before—the pioneers who built homes along the Missouri River, the railroad workers who never made it home, the children whose lives were cut short far too soon. Their spirits remind us that history isn't just dates in textbooks, but *real* people whose hopes, dreams, and sometimes unfinished business live on. Somewhere in this historic town, Sallie might be playing with her toys, the Lady in Black might be checking on restaurant servers, and maybe—just maybe—Amelia Earhart's adventurous spirit is still soaring through her childhood home.

After all, in Atchison, Kansas, the dead never *really* say goodbye.

BROOKE MONTOYA loved reading scary stories as a child. Now she writes them about her real-life adventures as a paranormal investigator. Brooke travels the nation looking for scary adventures to prove ghosts exist. She is also a counselor and teacher living in Oklahoma. While she is writing, she enjoys snuggles from her two dogs, Velvet and Nova. Visit www.brookemontoya.com to learn more!

Check out some of the other *Spooky America* titles available now!

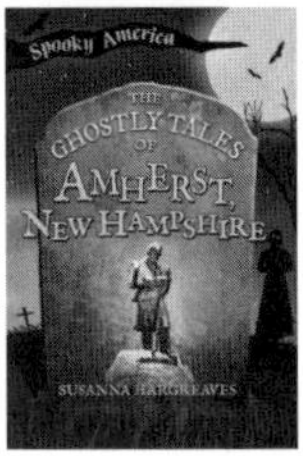

Spooky America was adapted from the creeptastic *Haunted America* series for adults. *Haunted America* explores historical haunts in cities and regions across America. Here's more from the original *Haunted Atchison* author, Brooke Montoya:

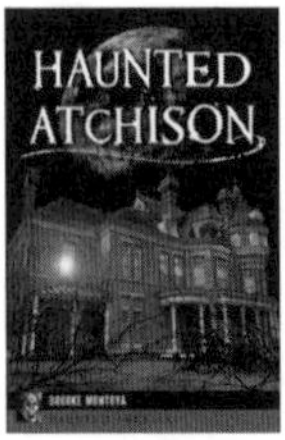